A New True Book

OZONE HOLE

By Darlene R. Stille

CHILDRENS PRESS®
CHICAGO

Cars, trucks, and buses are a
major source of air pollution.

PHOTO CREDITS

AP/Wide World Photos—40 (top and bottom right)

© Cameramann International, Ltd.—2, 23 (right), 37 (top)

© Virginia R. Grimes—16 (bottom)

H. Armstrong Roberts—© R. Krubner, Cover; © Camerique, 14 (bottom), 18, 35

© Emilie Lepthien—21 (top right), 23 (left)

© Norma Morrison—12, 40 (bottom left)

Odyssey/Frerck/Chicago—© Robert Frerck, 6

Photri—22 (left), 24 (2 photos), 33, 43 (left)

Root Resources—10, © Irene Hubbell, 21 (bottom right); © L.E. Schaefer, 42

SuperStock International, Inc.—© Ernest Manewal, 11

TSW/CLICK-Chicago—8, 21 (left), 22 (right), 45; © John Lawlor, 13 (top); © Gerard Fritz, 13 (center); © Billy E. Barnes, 14 (top); © Terence Harding, 26; © Leonard Lee Rue, 43 (right)

Valan—4, © Aubrey Diem, 13 (bottom); © Phillip Norton, 15, 44 (left); © Albert Kuhnigk, 16 (top); © V. Wilkinson, 36 (2 photos), 37 (bottom left and right), 39 (2 photos); © Tom W. Parkin, 44 (right)

COVER: Smog, Los Angeles, California

Library of Congress Cataloging-in-Publication Data

Stille, Darlene R.
   The ozone hole / by Darlene R. Stille.
      p.   cm. — (A New true book)
   Includes index.
   Summary: Studies the important role of atmospheric ozone in protecting the Earth, and tells how man-made chemicals are causing worrisome holes in the polar ozone layers.
   ISBN 0-516-01117-0
   1. Chlorofluorocarbons—Environmental aspects—Juvenile literature.   2. Ozone layer depletion—Environmental aspects—Juvenile literature.
3. Ozone layer—Juvenile literature. [1. Ozone
2. Ozone layer.   3. Air—Pollution.] I. Title.
TD887.C47S75   1991   90-20843
363.73'84—dc20   CIP
                                                    AC

TABLE OF CONTENTS

The ozone layer high in the atmosphere protects
the earth from harmful rays from the sun.

TOO LITTLE
AND TOO MUCH

There is too little ozone high above the earth. Scientists say this is bad. And there is too much ozone close to the ground. Scientists say this is bad, too.

What do the scientists mean? How can this be? What is ozone? And why is it so important to us?

The clear, fresh air that we breathe is threatened by chemical pollution.

WHAT OZONE IS

Ozone is a gas. It is a close relative of the oxygen in the air that we breathe. Breathing oxygen is good for us. We could not live without oxygen. But breathing ozone can harm our lungs, and ozone in the air can harm our eyes.

Ozone and oxygen are both gases. They are invisible. We cannot see these gases.

We cannot smell oxygen. But sometimes we can smell

7

Ozone is made when the electric charge in a lightning
bolt comes in contact with the oxygen in the air.

ozone. Ozone has a sharp,
tangy smell. Sometimes you
can smell the ozone made
by an electric spark.
Sometimes you can smell
ozone in the air during a
thunderstorm. This ozone is
made by lightning.

"BAD" OZONE

Ozone can be bad for us or good for us, but there is only one kind of ozone. Whether it is bad for us or good for us depends on where the ozone is. Its location makes it either helpful or harmful to people.

Ozone is found in two locations. It is either high in the air—about 15 to 20 miles up—or close to the ground. Close to the ground,

9

PUBLIVIA

contaminación
un problema

una solución: su colaboración

muchos colaboran. ¿y usted?

Es un mensaje del Ayuntamiento de Madrid

This pollution-awareness sign in Madrid, Spain, tells people
that everyone must cooperate to solve the problem of pollution.
Opposite page: Increasing traffic on the world's roads and highways
causes more and more smog to appear over cities.

ozone is bad. In the air
around us—the air we
breathe—ozone is pollution.
Ozone pollution comes
mainly from automobile
exhausts.

11

Air pollution is a worldwide problem. United States cities, such as
New York (opposite) and Los Angeles (top, opposite), and foreign cities,
such as Tokyo, Japan (above), have severe smog. Even less crowded
areas such as the Rhône Valley (bottom, opposite) in Switzerland
have pollution problems.

Sunlight shining on ozone near the ground makes smog. Smog makes the air a brownish-yellow color. Smog makes people cough. It can make our eyes water. It can hurt our lungs. Breathing ozone in smog can even kill people who have lung diseases.

12

Solar Electric Powered Air Sampler

New Jersey Air Sampler Network

The State of New Jersey, Department of Environmental Protection operates more than one hundred of these air samplers throughout the State. The object of this network of samplers is to monitor the quality of the air we breathe.

The air sampler operates for 24 hours every sixth day. Air is drawn through a glass fiber filter like those below and minute particles of polluting substances are trapped and held for later examination.

The information obtained from these samples allows the State to determine whether Air Quality Standards are being met and to measure our progress in controlling air pollution.

Sample Filters

New   Used   Used
             good air   dirty air

Electricity From The Sun

This photovoltaic, or solar cell, power system generates electricity from sunlight in a quiet, simple, and non-polluting manner.

The system consists of a solar array, controls and a storage battery. The solar cells in the array above convert sunlight directly to electricity. The controls channel the electricity to an air sampler located in the cylindrical structure to your left, and to a storage battery located inside this structure. The battery stores electricity to provide power at night and on cloudy days. Performance of the system is displayed by the meters above.

This installation demonstrates one of many practical applications of solar electricity. Small solar electric systems, such as you see here, now power forest lookouts in northern California and several remote weather stations throughout the United States, while larger systems provide power to the Papago Indian village of Schuchuli, Arizona and the village of Tangaye in Upper Volta, Africa.

Air Sampler   Instruments/Controls   Batteries   Solar Array

Scientists use monitoring equipment to measure the levels of air pollution in cities (opposite page) and in rural areas (above). Computerized vans (inset, opposite page) carry the monitoring equipment to local areas of pollution.

On days when there is lots of ozone in the air, the local weather service may issue an ozone alert. People who have breathing problems are warned to stay indoors.

Even healthy people should not run or play or work too hard outdoors when there is an ozone alert.

Sunlight contains
ultraviolet rays
that are harmful
to life. But
these rays are
blocked out by
the ozone layer
high above the earth.

16

"GOOD" OZONE

High in the atmosphere, ozone is good for people. There is a natural ozone layer in the air high above the earth.

This ozone layer acts like sunglasses for the earth. It blocks out harmful rays from the sun. There are many kinds of rays in sunlight. Some are visible light rays.

Exposure to ultraviolet rays can cause severe burning and even skin cancer in humans.

Some rays are invisible and harmful ultraviolet, or UV, rays.

Ultraviolet rays can cause skin cancer in humans. UV rays can harm animals.

These rays can also kill the tiny creatures in the ocean that fish feed on.

The ozone layer in the atmosphere blocks out these UV rays. The ozone layer keeps most of these harmful rays from reaching the earth's surface. Without the ozone layer, life on earth would not be possible.

THE INVISIBLE OZONE HOLE

Today, scientists are worried about earth's ozone layer. They say there is a hole in the ozone. This hole is above Antarctica near the South Pole.

Scientists are worried that UV rays coming through this hole will harm life in Antarctica. They are worried about the penguins. They

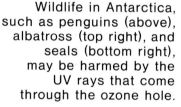

Wildlife in Antarctica,
such as penguins (above),
albatross (top right), and
seals (bottom right),
may be harmed by the
UV rays that come
through the ozone hole.

are worried about the seals
and birds and fish and small
sea animals.

They are also worried that
the hole will get bigger. They
are afraid it might grow and

21

Scientists in Antarctica (left) prepare for a flight of an airplane that will measure the gases in the atmosphere. Divers (right) check the icy Antarctic waters for pollution.

spread over South America. And they are afraid that another hole might be forming in the ozone over the Arctic Circle near the North Pole.

But ozone is invisible. So how did the scientists find a hole in something they can't see?

HOW TO FIND
AN INVISIBLE HOLE

Scientists have special instruments that measure invisible gases. They attach these instruments to huge weather balloons, and they

A weather balloon (left) will rise high in the air, and a scientist (below) will receive data about atmospheric gases from the instruments carried by the balloon.

send the balloons high into the atmosphere. When the huge balloons come down, the instruments tell the scientists what kinds of gases are up there.

Sometimes the scientists use airplanes. They attach

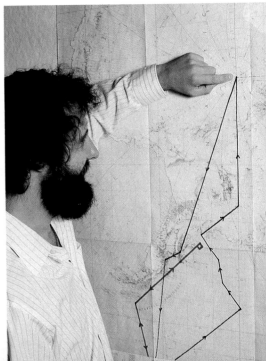

A scientist examines satellite data (below) on atmospheric data and plots a course (right) for an airplane that will carry instruments to measure gases in the air.

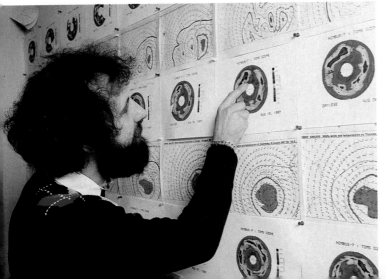

their measuring instruments to the planes. Then, as the planes fly through the atmosphere, the instruments measure the gases.

Scientists have been measuring gases above Antarctica for many years. Over time, the scientists noticed a change. The instruments showed that there was less and less ozone.

Molecules are much too small to see. They are made of two or more atoms joined together. The molecules that make up ozone and the molecules that make up the oxygen we breathe are both made up of oxygen atoms. Two oxygen atoms make an oxygen molecule. Three oxygen atoms make an ozone molecule.

THIS IS THE OXYGEN WE BREATHE

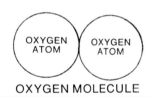

OXYGEN MOLECULE

THIS IS THE OZONE IN THE AIR

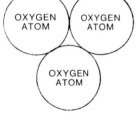

OZONE MOLECULE

UV rays strike oxygen molecules high in the atmosphere and break them apart into two separate oxygen atoms. The UV rays also break up ozone molecules. The ozone molecules are broken into a two-atom oxygen molecule and one free atom of oxygen Ozone molecules break up more easily than oxygen molecules.

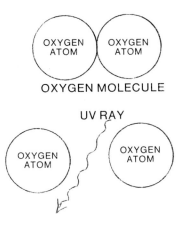

OXYGEN MOLECULE

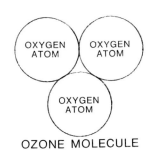

OZONE MOLECULE

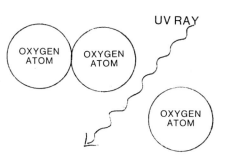

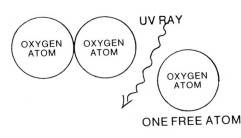

ONE FREE ATOM

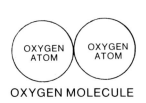

OXYGEN MOLECULE

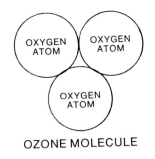

OZONE MOLECULE

When oxygen and ozone molecules are broken up, single oxygen atoms are left in the atmosphere. When two of these free oxygen atoms come together again, they join to make a molecule of oxygen. When three oxygen atoms come together, they create a molecule of ozone.

So in the atmosphere, ozone is always being created and destroyed. Normally, this natural cycle is in perfect balance. It keeps just the right amount of ozone in the ozone layer.

But now the scientists could see that something was destroying the ozone faster than nature could make it. What could that "something" be?

FINDING THE "SOMETHING" THAT DESTROYS OZONE

Whatever is destroying the ozone layer must be something quite new, the scientists realized. There must be something in the atmosphere that was not there before.

They looked for that "something" in air pollution. They tested the artificial chemicals found in air pollution. They learned that

some of these chemicals
help UV rays destroy ozone
very much faster.

Now scientists think that a
certain group of chemicals
are the main cause of the
ozone hole. These chemicals
are called chlorofluorocarbons,

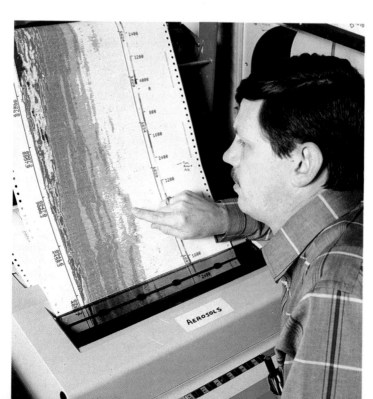

A scientist examines
chemical data being
sent from an
airplane flying
through the atmosphere.

or CFCs. UV rays and CFC molecules break up ozone very quickly.

The atoms that break off from one CFC molecule can destroy up to 100,000 ozone molecules! And CFCs can stay in the atmosphere for more than 100 years.

HOW TO SAVE "GOOD" OZONE

The only way to save the ozone is to stop sending CFCs into the atmosphere. The scientists know where the CFCs come from.

They come from air conditioners. They come

Chlorofluorocarbons (CFCs) are used in air conditioners. This man is repairing an air conditioner's condensing unit.

Plastic-foam containers for fast food and plastic foam, used in supermarkets to package vegetables (left) and meat (right), are a major problem.

from some cleaning fluids. They come from fast-food containers made of plastic foam. And they come from some kinds of spray cans.

CFCs should no longer be used in these products. Air conditioners should not be

Spray cans that contain CFCs (above) may harm the ozone layer. Ozone-safe cans (left and below) do not contain CFCs.

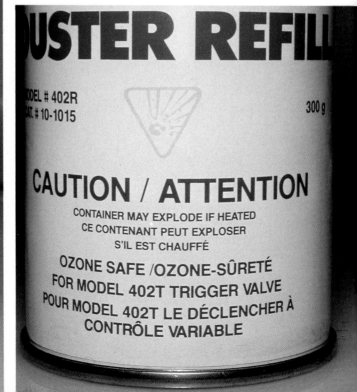

thrown away. Instead, the chemicals inside them should be recycled. Hamburgers and other foods should not be sold in plastic-foam boxes. They should be wrapped in paper.

Plastic-foam hamburger containers (above) are being replaced
by paper wrappers (below) to save the ozone layer.

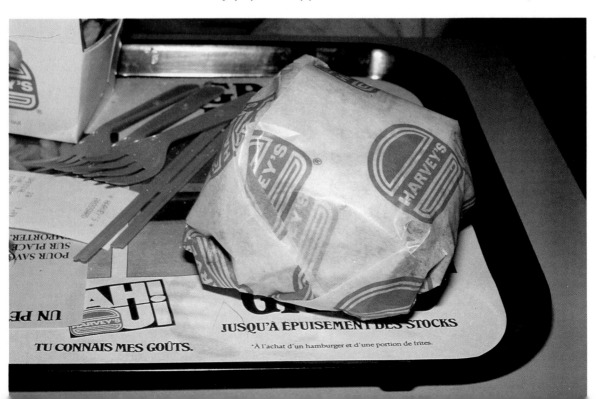

A sign on a street in Tokyo (bottom
left) gives readings for air pollutants.
People in smoggy cities (above
and below) wear masks on days
when pollution levels are high.

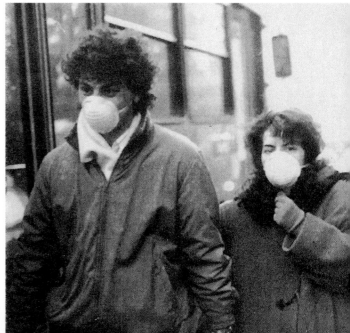

Spray cans containing CFCs should be banned. They are already banned in the United States. But people still use them in other parts of the world.

Closing the ozone hole is a problem that concerns all the nations of the world. All the people on earth must work together to solve this problem.

Living things depend on clean, fresh air to survive.

GETTING RID OF "BAD" OZONE

We must save the good
ozone high in the atmosphere.
And we must get rid of the
bad ozone near the ground.

Ozone near the ground cannot travel up into the atmosphere, because other chemicals and sunlight destroy it first. So we must stop the air pollution that causes ozone near the ground.

A haze of smog over Johannesburg, South Africa (left). Mexico City (right) has a very bad smog problem because surrounding mountains keep winds from blowing pollution away.

Some cars (left) run on propane,
a cleaner fuel than gasoline.
A filling station in Canada (above)
advertises natural gas vehicle fuel.

Scientists are trying to
make better fuel for cars.
Some kinds of fuels produce
much less ozone.

There is too much ozone
near the ground. And there is
too little ozone high in the

We must all work together to keep our beautiful planet free from pollution.

air. These are two different problems, but they are two of the biggest problems for our environment today. Scientists and other people are working very hard to solve them.

WORDS YOU SHOULD KNOW

artificial (ahr • tih • FISH • il) — made by people; not natural

atmosphere (AT • muss • fear) — the layer of air that is all around the earth

atom (AT • um) — any of the tiny particles that make up the chemical elements

chemicals (KEHM • ih • kilz) — materials that are used in fertilizers and in many manufacturing processes and that are often harmful to living things

chlorofluorocarbons (klor • oh • floo • roh • CAR • bunz) — chemicals containing the elements chlorine and fluorine that are used in some products and processes

cycle (SY • kil) — a complete set of events that keeps happening in the same order

environment (en • VYE • ron • mint) — all the things that surround something; air, soil, water, etc.

exhaust (ex • AWST) — gases that are given off by automobiles when gasoline is incompletely burned

gas (GASS) — a substance that is not solid or liquid, but is fluid and able to expand indefinitely

instruments (IN • struh • ments) — tools or machines used for scientific work such as measuring or weighing

invisible (in • VIH • zih • bil) — not capable of being seen; not visible

molecule (MAHL • ih • kyool) — the smallest particle of a substance that can exist and still keep its chemical form

oxygen (AHX • ih • jin) — a gas that is found in the air and that humans and animals need to breathe

ozone (OH • zohn) — a special form of oxygen that is harmful to people

pollution (puh • LOO • shun) — the dirtying of the air, soil, or water

smog (SMAWG) — a polluted haze formed when sunlight acts on the gases put into the air by automobile exhausts

ultraviolet rays (uhl • tra • VY • lit RAYZ) — rays from the sun that are beyond the range of visible light and that can be harmful to living things

INDEX

About the Author

Darlene R. Stille is a Chicago-based science writer and editor.